PETS AND PESTS

Contents

Jed and the Sheepdog — page 2

Pampered Pooches — page 14

Claire Llewellyn

Story illustrated by Steve May

Before Reading

In this story

 Jed

 The dog

Tricky words

- note
- smelled
- brushed
- hair
- scratched
- fleas
- jumped
- why

Introduce these tricky words and help the reader when they come across them later!

Story starter

Jed's mum is a vet. She looks after sick animals. Sometimes she keeps an animal overnight at her home. One day, Mum had to go out. She left a note for Jed asking him to brush the dog.

Jed and the Sheepdog

Jed looked at the note.

Jed looked at the dog.

The dog looked bad.
It smelled bad too.

Jed brushed the dog.
He brushed and brushed.

Hair came out of the dog …
lots and lots of hair.

The dog scratched.
It scratched and scratched.

Jed looked at the dog.

Fleas came out of the dog ... lots and lots of fleas.

The dog jumped in the pond.

The fleas jumped off the dog!

Where do you think the fleas will go?

Jed brushed the dog.

The dog looked good.
It smelled good too.

Mum came out and looked at the dog.

"The dog looks good," said Mum.

"But why are you scratching?" said Mum.

Quiz

Text Detective

- What happened when Jed brushed the dog?
- What went wrong with Jed's plan to get rid of the dog's fleas?

Word Detective

- **Phonic Focus:** Final letter sounds
  Page 4: Find a word that ends with the phoneme 'g'.
- Page 5: Can you find the word 'brushed' three times?
- Page 8: What words did Jed say?

Super Speller

Read these words:

came   why   go

Now try to spell them!

HA! HA! HA!

Q What's the difference between a dog and a flea?

A A dog can have fleas but a flea can't have dogs!

Before Reading

Find out about

- How some dog owners pamper their dogs

Tricky words

- many
- people
- friend
- owners
- fancy
- birthday
- invite
- hotel

Introduce these tricky words and help the reader when they come across them later!

Text starter

Many dog owners like to buy presents like fancy collars for their dogs. Some even have birthday parties for their dogs. Their dog is their best friend.

Pampered Pooches

Many people have dogs.

Their dog is their best friend.

Some dog owners buy presents for their dogs.

They buy their dogs fancy collars.

This collar is made of diamonds!

They buy them coats.

They even buy them fancy dress!

Some owners buy birthday presents for their dogs.

They have a birthday party for their dogs.

They invite some dogs to the party.

They even buy their dogs a birthday cake!

Some owners take their dogs to a dog hotel.

The dogs have a make-over.

Some dogs even look like their owners.

Or do the owners look like their dogs?

Quiz

Text Detective

- What sorts of things do some dog owners do on their dog's birthday?
- Do you know anyone who dresses their dog in clothes?

Word Detective

- **Phonic Focus:** Final letter sounds
  Page 17: Find a word that ends with the phoneme 'm'.
- Page 17: Can you find the word 'buy' twice?
- Page 18: Can you find a word made up of two smaller words?

Super Speller

Read these words:

for   do   the

Now try to spell them!

HA! HA! HA!

Q What do you get when you cross a cocker spaniel, a poodle and a rooster?

 A cocka-poodle-doo!